THE PORT

SERIES TITLES

Another Native Tongue
Susan Riley Clarke

Torrential
Jayne Marek

Users with Access: New and Selected Poems
Brandon Krieg

Dining on Salt: Four Seasons of Septets
Wayne Lee

Flu Season
Katrina Kalisz

No Trouble Staying Awake
Teresa Scollon

Catch & Release
Lauren Crawford

Steelhead
Lauren K. Carlson

The Coronation of the Ghost
Benjamin Gantcher

The Stone Tries to Understand the Hands
Susannah Sheffer

Red Camaro
Dwaine Rieves

Where Babies Come From
Ori Fienberg

Cuttings
Hannah Dow Kombiyil

Forgive the Animal
Sarah Pape

Love as Invasive Species
Ellen Kombiyil

They Were Horrible Cooks
Allison Whittenberg

The New Life
Wendy Wisner

Restoring Prairie
Margaret Rozga

Table with Burning Candle
Julia Paul

A Bright Wound
Sarah A. Etlinger

The Velvet Book
Rae Gouirand

Listening to Mars
Sally Ashton

Glitter City
Bonnie Jill Emanuel

The Trouble with Being a Childless Only Child
Michelle Meyer

Happy Everything
Caitlin Cowan

Dear Lo
Brady Bove

Sadness of the Apex Predator
Dion O'Reilly

Do Not Feed the Animal
Hikari Miya

The Watching Sky
Judy Brackett Crowe

Let It Be Told in a Single Breath
Russell Thorburn

The Blue Divide
Linda Nemec Foster

Lake, River, Mountain
Mark B. Hamilton

Talking Diamonds
Linda Nemec Foster

Poetic People Power
Tara Bracco (ed.)

The Green Vault Heist
David Salner

There is a Corner of Someplace Else
Camden Michael Jones

Everything Waits
Jonathan Graham

We Are Reckless
Christy Prahl

Always a Body
Molly Fuller

Bowed As If Laden With Snow
Megan Wildhood

Silent Letter
Gail Hanlon

New Wilderness
Jenifer DeBellis

Fulgurite
Catherine Kyle

The Body Is Burden and Delight
Sharon White

Bone Country
Linda Nemec Foster

Not Just the Fire
R.B. Simon

Monarch
Heather Bourbeau

The Walk to Cefalù
Lynne Viti

The Found Object Imagines a Life: New and Selected Poems
Mary Catherine Harper

Naming the Ghost
Emily Hockaday

Mourning
Dokubo Melford Goodhead

Messengers of the Gods: New and Selected Poems
Kathryn Gahl

After the 8-Ball
Colleen Alles

Careful Cartography
Devon Bohm

Broken On the Wheel
Barbara Costas-Biggs

Sparks and Disperses
Cathleen Cohen

Holding My Selves Together: New and Selected Poems
Margaret Rozga

Lost and Found Departments
Heather Dubrow

Marginal Notes
Alfonso Brezmes

The Almost-Children
Cassondra Windwalker

Meditations of a Beast
Kristine Ong Muslim

PRAISE FOR
Another Native Tongue

Susan Riley Clarke's *Another Native Tongue* is a gift. Clarke's poems dazzle, her voice luminescent, holding all that she loved into the light: from the speaker's mother drifting across the grass, to her daughter, still young…her flute clear and vivid as black confetti against blue. There's abundance—a lush music here—Clarke poignant and brave in the turns she takes—embracing the challenges, celebrating the "astonishing flight" of a fully lived life. We stand with the poet enraptured by the movements of the hummingbird: How many times left/ to see their wings pivot like wrists—/their glittering belly, emeralds,/ moving through air/, like water/like dolphins,/born with gifts of/astonishing flight. This is a book to hold close, a "native tongue" to celebrate, poems that will stay with us, poems that bring home the true purpose of a poem.

—CAROL POTTER
author of *What Happens Next is Anyone's Guess*

Another Native Tongue by Susan Riley Clarke is a rich collection of deeply moving poems that enter the reader's soul, lamenting and loving through themes bound up with a tender influence of place and time. This poignant glimpse into the complicated life of the poet is filled with astounding images and language that lingers long after, filling one with a sense of renewed wonder for the complexity of a life lived without blinders—honestly and openly. Clarke's poems capture all that is often hidden in our shadow selves, bravely revealed in these intimate moments of babies and beaches, motherhood and misogyny, loneliness and longing. This collection is a tribute to a brilliant poet and kinder friend, and a must-read for all who desire an authentic life, no matter the cost.

—ANNE M. DICHELE
author of *Ankle Deep and Drowning*

Susan and I once wrote in a group together. When she read aloud, everything grew still. One gem after another poured from her pen. Susan knew what she was doing, even with first drafts. How I longed to be that gifted! This glorious collection you hold in your hands will be a blessing to you. If you too are a poet, pay close attention to her artistry. Maybe you can learn a thing or two—not just about crafting a poem, but about living an authentic life, pain and all.

—JAN FRAZIER
author of *The Great Sweetening: Life After Thought*

In Susan Riley Clarke's posthumous collection, there is an insistence on telling the story, on preserving memories of places and of people. These are intensely personal poems which also remind us of the universal experiences of loss, change, and joy. Full of finely wrought details from the world as we know it—the smell of leaves burning, the image of a field of vivid loosestrife—the poems also contain elements of fairy tales and ghosts. In fact, Clarke herself is a ghost whose story becomes a mirror for us still navigating this plane. The result is a memoir-esque book that immerses us in all stages of the poet's life from a childhood of drive in movie theaters and Kodak slide carousels, to a young adulthood played out against a background of Joni Mitchell's lyrics, through childrearing and caretaking years, and finally to the place where the poet contemplates her own aging. "I'm chasing time around the stove," she writes. But then, so are we. Despite the acknowledgement of time's relentless surge, these haunting and evocative poems are filled with the light of snowfields, stars, fireflies, the white confetti of apple blossoms. Clarke reminds us that this world, no matter its imperfections, is a beautiful place in which to spend a lifetime.

—CARLA PANCIERA
author of *Barnflower: A Rhode Island Farm Memoir*

ANOTHER NATIVE TONGUE

selected poems

Susan Riley Clarke

edited by
Megan Hart & Rebecca Kinzie Bastian

Cornerstone Press, Stevens Point, Wisconsin 54481
Copyright © 2025 Megan Hart
www.uwsp.edu/cornerstone

Printed in the United States of America by
Point Print and Design Studio, Stevens Point, Wisconsin

Library of Congress Control Number: 2025932475
ISBN: 978-1-960329-80-6

All rights reserved.

Cornerstone Press titles are produced in courses and internships offered by the Department of English at the University of Wisconsin–Stevens Point.

DIRECTOR & PUBLISHER
Dr. Ross K. Tangedal

EXECUTIVE EDITORS
Jeff Snowbarger, Freesia McKee

EDITORIAL DIRECTOR
Brett Hill

SENIOR EDITOR
Ellie Atkinson

PRESS STAFF
Karlie Harpold, Allison Lange, Sophie McPherson, Ava Willett, Madison Schultz, Autumn Vine

for Megan and Joshua

FOREWORD

Editing a book is always a privilege. The process is intimate, meticulous, loving. But this was something more. Susan Riley Clarke left this plane of existence before her work was assembled in any formal way; she didn't leave a manuscript, or collection, just scraps of writing, poems published in literary journals, and word documents in no particular order. Incredibly, in the midst of her own grief, her daughter, Megan Hart, started sorting and collecting every bit of her mother's writing she could find—journal pages, handwritten notes, magazines, computer files—and put them together in a tender pile for me to arrange and edit, a process that felt mystical and spiritual in a way I had never experienced before. I have found new friends, new sisters, in this process, one gone, one left to carry on. Both wise, strong, heart-driven. Both teachers, mothers, explorers.

The resulting book is a love letter. A story of generations; a memory song; a tribute to time, change, loss, the way this earth both includes and spins away from us. It is a celebration of life. Susan's writing is lyrical, muscular, evocative. Her striking voice stays true, year after year, and tells the story of her mother, her children, her own life, like a timeless fable we recognize and participate in. The professor in her is also at work here, insisting on precision and clarity in the midst of the magic. Megan and I have been left tearful and exhilarated by *Another Native Tongue* and you will too. Read with reverence and an open heart.

—Rebecca Kinzie Bastian
January 2025

CONTENTS

Foreword	xv
Fall Again	1

I.

Approach of the Forest Animals	5
Divine Intrusion	6
Hummingbird	7
Holding the Moon	8
The Interview	9
Selling the Cape	10
At Kenyon July 24	12
Georgia O'Keefe	13
Dream	14
For John Lennon	15
I Am Afraid	16
Epiphany	17
In the Upper Room	18
In Memoriam	20
After the Resurrection	21
End of August	22
Middle-Aged in Bonducci's Café	23
A True Story about a Tree	24
Partial Memory	25
Ex Libris John Riley	28

II.

A Woman Runs and Runs	31
Spring Again	32
I Wish I'd Called You Honey	34
Train Platform	35
Apple Tree	36
Sweet Corn	37
Loosestrife	38
In the Old House	39
Beach Houses	40
Reunion	42
Summer Falling Down	43
Couplet Practice	44
Mary of the Lake, 1970	45
Ode to a Frying Pan	46
Family Counseling for the Montagues and Capulets	47
Fireflies	48
First Marriage	50
Leaving the Followers	51
I Wander	52
Sanctum	53
Women Writers	55
Mountain Legend	56
Lights	57

III.

Elegy for Laverne	61
In the Beginning	62
For David and Megan	63
Letting Go	65
For Nickels and Candy	66
Advice For My Teenager	67
Amherst in Perspective	68
Barn Cats at Big Meadow Creek	69
For Sylvia Plath	70
After Easter	71
Spring Drowning	72
Missing	73
Ode to Losartan	74
You Know	75
Trespasser	76
Sacrificial Rites	77
Leaving P'town Before the Parade	79
A Change in Luck	80
Off Across the Bay	81
You Linger	82
Time of Death	83
Acknowledgments	85

Fall Again

This time of year
when it's gold like this,
I am flushed, red
swirling, feverish to change.
A song on the car radio,
the orange disc of sun in the rear-view mirror,
remind me of hills
I had intended to reach all summer
but caught myself, like a snag in my stocking
here in this seat belt instead.
Once more, my yard is buried in leaves.
The back door flies wide open in the wind.
I hear geese wailing about some odyssey,
their black-dotted trail across the sky
pointing a huge arrow
towards a turn, a different name,
another native tongue.

1.

Approach of the Forest Animals

My mother looks from the window for forest animals.
She listens, her head a fertile ground
for cancer seeding, spreading its network,
rooting through memories
and all the arguments of the past.
In a sudden clearing, she sees them:
chipmunks come from under the porch,
squirrels on the roof above her
drop chestnuts and stars from their mouths;
from the hot, green woods tiptoes the stray orange cat;
birds whirl toward her red bee balm.
From distant brush comes the proud brown deer,
walks towards the house, stares in.
All the animals are coming close;
their footprints cover her garden, steps to the porch;
their breath fills her living room.
It's the forest animals, the ones
she opens a wide glass door for in her dreams.
They listen, too, to her secrets from the time she lived
alone, young, and unafraid.
Shall I turn back to the time I was unafraid?
Go over the confusing parts, make them smooth,
squeeze out the thorns?
I will tell them my story, the one
I carried through a lifetime,
now, when everyone has gathered,
the nurses and the children and the animals.
I will set it out as I knew it,
and there will be no argument.

Divine Intrusion

If I lived in that transparent house
of open windows filled with green shade,
I'd write you love letters, long
rambles of what I did that day,
where I've stored my children's toys
in attic boxes, and how I don't need anything,
that I get through a day's work floating
in the physical company of spirits.
Ghost cats flick their ears with waiting,
hunt under a moon.
I watch them from my sleep,
eavesdrop on their conversations
that tell me someone is coming.
You walked invisibly
in front of me,
stopped
behind a woman who then fell.
I look for you in faces of those
who are looking for you.
I felt the palm of your hand
on the windowpane I stared through.
In that place you inhabit
there is nothing to need,
which is why it takes so long to find my way back,
stumbling on pebbles, words, the sound of your name.

Hummingbird

How many chances
do you think you have left
to see a stilled hummingbird
on the tip of a leaf,
its nest an artist's bowl,
grassbound with sticky spider silk—
to see her mate flex
iridescent feathers
a fiery flower,
to hear its mating chorus,
each with his own part to sing?
The song is just the beginning!

How many times left
to see their wings pivot like wrists—
their glittering belly, emeralds,
moving through air,
like water,
like dolphins,
born with gifts of
astonishing flight?

Holding the Moon

A neighbor is practicing Qigong in the woods.
Her arms sweep up towards the sky,
form a circle in the shape of the moon.
She stands still on one leg
like a marsh bird, her whole body
breathing in, breathing out.
She bends at the waist,
swoops down, a snowy egret,
into an imaginary wetland.
At a table by the window
my mother sits watching her.
My mother can't form words now,
has no weight to her,
not much time.
I take my mother's hand
and watch her staring through the glass
at the bird-like movements,
the sweeping arms,
and the round full moon between them.
How wonderful
to stand in the forest
dreaming of the sea, unmindful
of words, weight, time.

The Interview

She said when you turn fifty,
your poetry will dry to cracked leaves,
moth's wings. You won't fight,
and all the rivers' movements,
like gnashing boats making circles,
banging oarlocks, bow of one to stern of the other
will slow, recede, leave a gravel bed
where night animals poke with hooves,
troubled by the lack of water sounds.
It won't! I thought like a screen door slammed.
She looked out towards the back yard.
Things that must be done get done.
I used to write my poems, she said,
on my stomach in the dark.
My body went ahead of them to tangles of love.
Lights went on in the middle of the night.
But I've compromised. Daily work goes on, now,
I've made my peace.
With what? I whispered across the table.
From her window, I watched leaves
looking like empty paper
whirl brown into still corners
where air could not lift them,
between stone walls, gutters,
the steps that lead out back.

Selling the Cape

I am leaving the towels on the line.
My mother will stay till fall,
her chair on the deck facing water
and pink sun falling to the gold September marsh.
I'm leaving the beach.
Every year the water laps closer
to asphalt, the strip of sand more narrow.
I have a photo of you in 1963,
a dot of black, the rest a stretch of tawny shore.
We are letting the plum roses spill in the wind.
The ones beside the door toppled over this year.
I won't bother with them now, my mother said.
She used to rinse my children's sandy feet
with her garden hose. She used to rinse mine, too.
She used to take long walks all the way to the cove
where the seals were one spring.
A few years ago, the hurricane
washed the sandy spit at Chatham out to sea,
and the house out on the dunes at Marconi
is gone.

I am letting the ocean go.

What will you do with the old red dresser?
We bought it for thirty dollars,
chipped paint over pine.
How will it look without honeysuckle
here in the window beside it,
the sun-browned baby laughing in the mirror?
But my baby is twenty.
He can carry it to the van on his back.

I am watching my little girl's skinny legs
scurry in and out of white ocean foam like the terns.
I am making a check through empty rooms,

my children's beach toys scattered into corners
of my thinking they are still two and four
on a sunny day at Skaket,
where I'd chase them and scoop them up
along the little bayside waves.

We'd walk through fields we could see the ocean from,
down sandy roads where you'd never pass a car,
never see lights at night
except from the stars, a few trawlers out at sea,
or from one late jeep in the dunes,
its headlights bouncing up and down
along the dark end-of-summer sky.

At Kenyon July 24

My mother died last July, a year ago today.
It seems the time that placed itself
between her face and now was very slow.
To realize she's gone is slower still.
In this Ohio summer woodchucks and blackbirds
take long days for granted.
Faith stares at me from the middle of the road.
In the window of the church, I see my mother
drift, loiter,
take her own sweet time crossing the grass.
She lifts one foot like a crow,
then another,
and flaps wide, lumbering wings.

Georgia O'Keefe

What was the pitch high-rushed
around sockets of the beast
without brown? What did you hear
in blanched oils, sharp splinters of jaw?
A cow stares in blue air:
years and years of dry heat
cleaved the skull.
The mouth went first.
Nothing frees us from light and wind.
A carcass stinks. Bones rise.
Our scaffolding
clatters over the hollow earth.
Rattle rattle. We are not our bodies.

Dream

From a ladder down to soggy mud
cellar walls half gone, open to tidal flats
otherworld grey, antediluvian,
I saw the one house to inhabit
on a hill clustered with houses,
pebbled roads ribboned around them—
I know it was where my mother lived.
From its highest window,
I could see the ferry leave
over churling, frantic waves.
Too late
to warn about the flood,
how it would need to fly,
how foundations would be broken through
to meet the whole shore's floor.

For John Lennon

*Now they know how many holes
it takes to fill the Albert Hall.*

—The Beatles, "A Day in the Life"

I wrote you something, but
I put the paper somewhere in my mouth.
He showed me where to look, the dentist,
after the hard-pressed pump, pump
up to the mirror, the bright, circular light.
There is so much food in here,
back of this one, around all these jetties,
white clods. Open.
The word holes, the places where
sentences are kept, are dirty.

I keep having dreams
of throwing out bath water.
What would you say to a comedian in an elevator?
That I've lived 13, 376 days?

Polymer scientists want to put a road
through my Victorian living room to their garage.
This is where I stand, Albert:
In the middle of a simulated birdcage game.
I am the cat watching feathers
blown by the wind of an electric fan.
One this way past my eyes,
one over my head.

I'd catch one, but my mouth is full of dentist's tools.
So many cavities.
So many feathers flying.

I Am Afraid

of losing air
a bird lost in a black mine
wet matches
dead car batteries
heat waves,
thieves, loose in the house.
I am afraid
end-of-summer winds
will rip tomatoes from their spine;
that I'll pass you in a grocery store
forgetting you're my son.
I am afraid I've lost
the tin of old buttons
where I keep my passport.
I am afraid
I'll stop hearing
the full matter of your laughter;
that I'll become a rickety cart
full of unbalanced weight;
that I'll carry unbalanced weight
down a staircase
without railings.
I am afraid
I'll lose the dream I had last night,
the purpose of a poem,
and of everything
I need.

Epiphany

Sky bleeds beneath the gilded door.
In its square glass, clouds fly against stars,
fly against black night.
The wood, the thick panels, are
glossy with centuries of silky paint,
gold brush strokes over cascades,
rococo labyrinths, flowers.
Remember the creak of seagoing timbers,
the huge ship that carried
the young cargo, clean ash
carved in sharp relief.
The hanging of it was cumbersome.
I can still hear
the slow moaning into place,
the tight vacuum in the shut.
It will store civilizations, revolutions,
colors, space.
When the wedding happens,
those who pass through
breathe water, swallow air.

In the Upper Room

As if from a faraway boat
fishing line looped through galaxies
cloaked in black infinity,
swirls of fiery stars.
The line anchored in our flesh,
tore through our bodies,
jump-started hearts,
like batteries on frogs' legs,
positive, negative, electric ice.
We choked up salt water,
breathed air mouth to mouth, soul to soul,
light from light, true God from true God,
seen and not heard, heard
without knowing. Someone
kicked over a chair.
The space of the room
filled with fruit.
We shared like a boat
shares waves in the sea,
one to another, mouth to mouth,
true God to true God.

How did we get to this place?
First we were shackled to monstrosities
then drawn, quartered and hung by hate…
Broken teeth and bones, stones
to the head…

And we bled out love,
anointing the sad, lonely world.

A bell tapped our foreheads.
Walls dissolved.
Infinity
filled us
with ghostly strength.

What was it to be there?
You were.
You must have drawn to your face
wafts of frankincense and myrrh.
You must have seen the fish.

You must have torn apart fields of bread.
You must have heard clattering mountains
begging to sing.

In Memoriam

You put a coin beneath your tongue
for passage; held hot coals
in your lips to speak with fire.
Why burn to embers
when a sound tongue can spill to jewels?

You take poems from the sides of roads
like the one to our house,
lit with chestnut blossoms,
and use language to feel your way home.

Your poems are like a child in a white nightgown
walking down the road at night with a dog.
Your poems are an angry buzzsaw
through to the core of a tree,
leaving a stump filled with circles.

I know where you've been,
with your sight arrested by stars.
I like your poems sweet,
with an aftertaste of honey.

But give me poems with teeth to mesh gears
groaning towards an awful war.
I took my poems to Flanders Field.
I wrote them when you died to mimic yours.
Here lies my father my poet my captain
who lied about the war to save our minds.

After the Resurrection

The grief of road-less-ness,
waterless canals,
the world wrung dry of sound,
mute dogs staring,
no clamor in the streets, banging on doors,
no shouting
like the day before.
Empty taste—
bitter and sweet gone to chaff like dead grain.
Clay would not hold.
Logic gone to the wind.
What had the stories been for?
We do not have to search: it will come to us.
We have to search: It will come to us.
In a dream, I fell through to unheard-of blue.
My fingers clenched a stone for ballast.
In the other hand
bread.

End of August

Old women are hacking brown weeds
out of thinning perennials
piling up the sidewalk outside a church.
I pull out dead stalks of
daylilies long turned from their hey,
long since colored trumpets,
not a nod of blue left in hydrangeas.
Four quail scud by the road
seem in a rush.
A hawk dives in front of my car.
Two goldfinches scold me from a branch above my head,
a pair of cardinals on the fence,
each step I take alongside,
they tweet to each other
about me.
What are you doing
following us along this perfect perching place,
this picket fence?

Middle-Aged in Bonducci's Café

In the booth next to me
a man asks the woman across the table
You have a relationship
with a transcendent being you call God?
She says *I like to think so.*
The steel coffee machine hisses out steamed milk.
Voices buzz, and a few minutes later,
it hisses again.
Lucky for me, I'm facing the street.
I don't have to figure out excuses
for the way they look.
I wonder, why so much black leather,
why the silver zippers, such high-heeled boots?
I'm still in a khaki raincoat and flats.
I have a picture of myself ten years ago
in a long, tan raincoat.
All they do here is pour coffee
to bumpy music I've never heard,
talk about their affairs with the cosmos,
slam thick ceramic mugs in plastic bins
on their way out the door.
In front of me, my reflection blurs
when a Peter Pan bus drives by.
There are more men here than in bars
back when I was looking.
But I never know the music they're playing
or why I pay so much for white foam.

A True Story about a Tree

A red-laced ornamental elm
poses long, thin arms,
a dancer
reaching for air, more light,
more reason
from the chaos of the sky.
Around her,
massive oaks
outweigh the possible sun,
hammer down
boisterous seeds
POP!
roof, car, cats,
the driveway to my house.
I need to cut down
their selfish green,
prune the dark
to make her outline sure,
her foothold strong
balance in the deep,
quickening landscape
on her own.

Partial Memory

When you left for good,
the hospital called to tell me
the news.
Now it's only me in this show.
Now who will tell me the stories
from before I was born?
The good news was
you'd kept photographs.
Clearing out your low-income
concrete cinder block housing,
I found them.

In one, I have my hand over my heart;
I'm looking at someone in the distance
I don't remember,
my hand as a pledge of allegiance
probably to you.

Who took the one
of our father between us,
my hand fluttering fingers
around my throat, maybe choking?

At Meg's wedding, you're telling me
something like the mother of the bride
shouldn't go up to people, you should
let them come to you; in another one,
you're telling Meg what to do.

At my wedding, someone took one of you
letting my two-year-old drop to the ground
after you'd tossed him in the air
like a doll.

For the early pictures, I need you now.
One of a waiter on an ocean liner to Italy,

who, carrying a high tray
of espresso cups and saucers,
had fallen down,
china scattered across the whole dining room floor;
and one of you in the swimming pool
of that same ship, when the ocean surrounding it
had turned in a sudden storm
to huge waves, the water in your pool
back and forth imitating
the entire sea.
You became the crest of the wave over the top of the pool,
beginning to rush back downwards toward its
bare concrete floor, your little girl legs frantic
as a turtle's, lifted by its shell.

Many photographs went missing;
some were estranged.
These we'd scrutinized under light,
but like reading a novel
you suspect you've read before
but not worth finishing
to remember how it ends, we let them drop
to the don't-know pile
like fingering a rosary in the dark,
each bead an unfocused slide.
Your life in living color was ephemeral,
an amusement ride, a whirly machine
that loses its floor
til we'd hang by gravity
to rubber walls
and scream.

Then there were the nameless people
in monochrome
from before I was born
(an anesthetized arrival).
I won't know who they were.
Who was this? I'd ask.

Where was this?
Before you let the ambulance
slouch towards Bethlehem,
I tried to lift your brain's ripples, shake them out
like your sheets, til the ones you'd forgotten
would get tossed up like gleeful babies
you'd recognize in mid-air and
yank them
back into the movie you were showing me.

Ex Libris John Riley

Now quiet swings this day to dark and ends
its function for all time. For many lying
still, it's been a noisy tumbril to
eternity. Both destination and conveyance
were unfair, but their complaints
are never heard by us. For those who live,
it was a time of light, short or long,
brightly etched upon the plates of our minds,
to be reproduced in later years,
prefaced by that solemn utterance:
"Now there was a day…"

2.

A Woman Runs and Runs

Lets blood out
runs it clear to water
running blood, running blood.
I'm chasing time
around
the stove where I pull
pans out burning around my head
and spring gnats
black dots whirling in streaks of sun
make my windows dirty.
I'm chasing you, time.
I've untied knots
opened latches, hinges
chased you through my kitchen, my parlor.
You run through my bed at night
like a wolf after caribou.
My legs churn in the sheets
kick away jaws at my heels, my thighs
my inner parts.
Time swirls down the chimney
whistles through my belly
flies at me
like herring dash against
 cold slippery rocks
somewhere
they try frantically
to go.

Spring Again

Spring, slow, don't go
                        too fast.
                              Don't turn to leaf too soon.

I waited long at iced windows
cracked against ever-black dark.
Only streetlights woke up mornings.
Winter clots the blood
is hard
to undo.
Spring, stay—
I waited lonesome
                for sun pale yellow on stone wall
                for daffodils to break brown ground
                for willow's closed silver toes of cat

                                    to pop white.

Even in March
both lion and lamb—

                (I grew tired with their coming and going)

plowed under snow.
Spring come home.

Let brave snowdrops bare green first
their flowered heads loop over
shy by
dead stump and cold fence.
Stay awhile.
The year made us
                so distant, so sparse
                        of hope of warm.

I need to
        see your face,
                spend time with you
                        now that you're back
again.

I Wish I'd Called You Honey

I wish I'd called you honey
like we got sweeties from Mother
and once in a while dears from Daddy
after we cried enough because of him.

No, I couldn't call you honey.
I could call you crazy for endearment.
I was the balloon holder
who clutched tight all the happy fliers
and colors to keep the business sane
sand in my shoes to keep the terra firma.

I'm the only one with the Styx River coins
to pay this one and that for the living you did.
I hope it pays the ferryman for your crossing, honey.
Call me when you get there.

Train Platform

When the war came into the station,
engine cursing, grinding steel,
we all put our children on board.
Father had a brown felt hat,
his broad chest squared in a formal suit.
Mother's red lips smiled under a netted veil.
She was pulling a hankie from her purse
to wipe lipstick from her little boy's cheek.
An address was pinned to his collar.

The whistle screamed *Terror! Terror!*
Up you go you, son!
Hot, loud blasts of grey smoke separated everyone.
I will never forget the little boy's body
scooped into the dark metal car, his arms
stretched out straight like a doll towards his mother,
nor the clatter of train
fading backward, fading backward,
catapulting into the horrible night.

Apple Tree

When I was small,
I climbed the apple tree out back,
high enough to see the house,
my mother hanging wash.
I slipped and tumbled
from the top.
Before I hit the ground,
a thick branch stub like a thumb
saved me by a belt loop in my shorts.
My arms and legs waved out in all directions
like a hanging doll.

In spring, that tree blossomed first:
pink chandeliers!
The orchard down the hill
would copy it,
turn pink itself, over and over in rows,
as if looking up, had seen the first light.

Some years past, the arm-like boughs
held nailed boards across their width
to make a secret place for our swinging legs
while we talked of boys,
or watched the distant farmer
weave through his orchard,
a tank on his back, spraying poison
to stay the worms, we thought,
to keep the young fruit whole.

Sweet Corn

We all crave the first crop,
dropped in brown bags by roadsides
like an airlift from the sky.
The early corn we had was plain,
but I am lonesome this summer;
I ate three ears, disappointing ones.
Feed for his cows, my sister said.
The farmer gave me extra with a wink.
Tonight's is a new batch.
Green husks and wisps of silky thread
lie all about the kitchen floor and patio.
Hot butter and steaming yellow sweets
wait on our plates.
Everyone bows in towards the table.
If it's good, we don't talk,
nod row after row,
become the animals,
startled by sugar.

Loosestrife

Upstate New York in August,
near Seneca Falls,
highways are deep purple with loosestrife.
For miles I drive along the sea of it,
roadsides a shore of green,
my car windows lit in fuchsia.
At home, it spread through wild fields
across the road from our house.
My father would shout from the window upstairs.
Come look at the *loosestrife!*
As if panic could stay the frantic waste of beauty,
spent too fast before saying what it meant.

In the summer, my father bellowed
up the street for my sister to come home.
He whistled for us, a sharp two-fingered blast:
We're going to the drive-in!
Clipped to the car door, the metal speaker
whined with mosquitoes and murmuring families,
station wagons tilted at a huge screen.

Sometimes, humid nights on our screened-in porch,
my father showed us colored slides
from the Kodak carousel. We'd see ourselves,
straight, sticky bodies in camp uniforms,
grinning in gaping teeth and ponytails.
There were slides he took of loosestrife, too,
deep rose and green, late August,
stilled for a moment in the hot, magnified light.

In the Old House

In October, we raked leaves at night,
burned them all along the stone wall.
I ran through the smoke, jumped over them,
the sky red and black and street-lit.
The cats ran alongside me,
all along the trees, glowing leaves
burning in my eyes, my father's eyes.
He dragged in more leaves,
the wind blew smoke dark orange,
my clothes smelled like ashes, ashes
in cold, smoky air.

Nights my father was away
we made candy,
pulled vanilla taffy in the kitchen
stretched long scalding sugar strings
between our fingers
till it hardened, like me,
hanging around the big white Westinghouse stove
wishing my mother loved me more.
She scraped hot fudge
from the bottom of the metal pot.
I scorched my tongue,
and my sister, her blouse too close to the burner,
caught on fire.

Beach Houses

Strung so close to each other
        we saw through windows
                end to end:
you at your morning table,
        a mother washing children's faces,
                flapping towels, shaking laundry;
                      a cat glaring from its perch on a sill.

In summer, a long, white curtain lifts with the wind,
        curls through your open window into mine,
                lies on the sill a moment like an envelope,
then slides back home.

If the houses were empty –
        say their people had gone to the beach –
                I could see through their windows
                      all the way to the water.

One late August you and I lay in the dunes, nose to nose.
        We saw our faces mirrored in the pupil of the other's eye
                before, like a camera's shutter,
we blinked.

Phones, too, were strung together in party lines.
        A phone rang in one house,
                someone answered in another.
                      By the time *war* was said,
                              everyone picked up their phone.

When war came across the ocean,
        we boarded windows, pulled towels from railings,
                left board games, pails and shovels,
                      a broken doll, a milk bottle gone sour.

If in our hurt confusion, we left windows open, doors ajar,
    sand would race through hollow houses, bank up in corners,
        rattle walls, and our not-knowing
            war could cross our ocean.

Its monsters would follow,
    splinter glass, rip doors off hinges,
        bulldoze kitchens, bury bedsprings,
            a clothespin....

Wild creatures kept at bay would be dominant.

I have one image I visit often:
    my face mirrored in the pupil of your eye –
        one late August, before
we blinked.

Reunion

In boarding school rituals,
we threw letters and diaries of broken hearts
into a fire at night.
Our confessions snapped and burned.
We sang school songs, too,
and hymns at Vespers, Sunday nights.
Weekends, we'd carry our laundry
up to washing machines at Smith College.
We wanted to be Smith College girls—
in Fair Isle sweaters, tweed skirts.
Smart, rich girls like Sylvia Plath,
who had walked around Paradise Pond,
her mind building difficult verses
of dangerous imagery in black.
We circled that pond, too, heady
with stories of love, poetry, and suicide,
a romance for our imagination,
at barely seventeen.

Summer Falling Down

after Joni Mitchell, "Urge for the Going"

We had sun-colored skin,
no one else but ourselves,
summer, its meadows and dunes.
We gobbled fish, champagne
coursed through our laughing throats.
Yes, I had sun-colored hair,
but restlessness came in with fall;
every bright thing was on its way out,
and you saying *stay another month or so
when green marshes turn gold*
scared me.
Days shortened,
cold shuttered all around us,
bullied me into leaving.
I'll miss the way you pulled covers to your chin
after you'd banked the beach fires
and bolted us in.

Now I'm stoned in a frat house,
a circle of kids smoking.
In my haze, I saw a ring you gave me,
hammered uneven from a silver dollar.
But I lost it. I lost the other ring, too,
and your frat pin with a tiny seed of pearl.
I had me a man in summertime

Steel guitars rang out pure, beautiful
loneliness.
A string of bare trees took note
and stiffened when I drove away.

Couplet Practice

For love of all past loves, I swear
I'd forfeit those of millionaires'
attention. Perhaps a car ride though,
shiny foreign swift and very low
to the ground—not missionary-
too crude—not necessary.
I'd relinquish that smug attention,
garish roses, rapid tongue, and not to mention
that ride through snowy woods at night,
top down, white breath, prematurely right
over my head. My overturned propriety,
my ladylike-ness, lost to notoriety.
I'd take back, though, the one I wore
a little white dress above the knees for,
for whom, that sweet country man
(in retrospect my Peter Pan)
I'd travel back in time's gnarled
channels, to schoolgirls gathered,
whirling damsels in dirndl skirts, singing
WASP-y hymns for grace, grades,
headmaster's whims.
I went from there, a dilettante to saboteur,
keeping those dark darling wolves from my door.

Mary of the Lake, 1970

Rushing from your baby-blue Ford
to noon mass glamorous
deliberate runaway
in high heels snakeskin dress sunglasses
hung over from country western dancing
big faith big hope big
map of Utopia

How it was then
was enormous change was
watershed spirit
deep glacial lake spirit
formed from chakras
wide open
We were all drawn in together
You swam up Grace Street shore
your entourage carrying knick-knacks
velvet couch lamps jewelry
We dried our hair feet hands
built odd chapels odd foundations
spoke new words new prayers
circled the bare floor
candles in the center
and Rose the vagabond cat

You were beautiful
(that snakeskin dress!)
By the time we shed old clothes
shared noisy rituals suppers wine
so many suitcases strangers from bus stations
Holy Ghost happenings
When we've been there ten thousand years
bright shining as the sun
the boats came
the ones on healing journeys
following clear water
only you had seen
from the beginning

Ode to a Frying Pan

When I went from Riley
to marry Murphy,
my mother,
New England-rooted Yankee,
warned:
Out of the frying pan, into the fire!
I jumped in.
A frying pan
heated to irrational anger
embattled bitter, Riley rage.
The frying pan, a metal club
for hitting cartoon heads:
not funny.
A gong
clanging troops back
to circle the fire,
to pay homage to the sturdy familiar
sitting sure over iron grates.
I am sure I am right.
My camp. My troops.
My rightful Irish rage.

Family Counseling for the Montagues and Capulets

We hate your entire race, my brothers said.
We'll annihilate yours, they shouted.
We drew straws: one boy from their side;
I took the other for a crazy dare.
Down behind the house, he took me,
kissed me til I lost my sense of purpose,
my family name.
We lied, bit lips, necks,
spilled ourselves over and over
on mother's sheets, his father's office floor.
If we're to die for them,
let our parents know we fornicate,
their pretty children.
Let them watch me ride Romeo like a sorceress,
the tip of his cock licking my dome like a flame.
To our families,
we leave our bodies, streaked with sweat and sacrilege.
To mine, a few summer days littered with childhood,
a ruin of pink and white pictures from the prom.
Keep the photos we had taken in cheap motels,
and the needles we were using
at the end.

Fireflies

> *Once in a while*
> *In a big blue moon,*
> *There comes a night like this,*
> *Like some surrealist*
> *Invented this*
> *4th of July…*
>
> —Joni Mitchell, "Night Ride Home"

That first night in the house by Cushman Brook,
streambed by our pillows, wobbly deck over tumbling water,
We're really in the country, you had said, a little afraid of the dark.
By early July, throughout the long yard into the woods,
tiny flashes lighted everywhere,
strands on Christmas tree branches,
jeweled spirits
sparkling above the lawn.
We lay in bed watching in the mirror,
their reflection between our toes,
holy motel neon signs:
Love me! Love me! Love me! Love me! Love me!
After the hot Fourth of July fireworks in town,
the smoke, banging blues, and traffic was finally still;
when bikes, families, and barking dogs settled down,
quiet came in like mist,
then crickets. Then lights in the damp grass
bubbled up like champagne.
We leaned in together watching.
That was some July.

Now I'm alone at dusk near the end of June,
in a clanging suburb. I see a flicker,
a baby pearl of light blinking.
Even here, in this thick neighborhood,
there will be fireflies.
But never those multitudes.

We had to wear bee netting into the yard that night,
so full of fireflies, it was bright as a full moon.
You always exaggerate, you'd accuse me.
But you wouldn't now.
You'll remember if you ever read this.
It was brilliant.
We were in a trance.
But we'd seen miracles before.

First Marriage

We lived on the West End
in between unhappiness. On summer nights
car motors rattled our bedroom screens.
Beer cans splashed open, hit our ceiling
as we lay staring up.
Irene, next door, fat and loud,
yelled at her husband and his friends. Yelled
all next day at their kids. She slapped
them silly.
On our other side,
a four-year-old lived alone.
Grey almond eyes, she twirled
along our porch banister, a paper
pinned to her dress. This is to phone
the police if I need to, she said.
Cruisers drove by, old couches out front,
blue TV light in the hot dark.
Everybody at the movies. They never
noticed us excuse ourselves from the mess
like we were going to move out any day.
I don't think they saw us, us being so white.
It must have surprised them,
my banging, dishes breaking against the wall.
But they knew what to do.
The knock at our door. The two-way radio
beeping in our front hall. I came
to the top of the stairs.
No, I'm fine.
I scream at him like this now.
I've lost my faith, sir, is all.

Leaving the Followers

What I remember was sand, rock hills, mountains,
caves, multitudinous, dry—
our silent bread baked on hot sacrificial stones,
where even a little tendril of vine
would have cried out to be saved.
Our plates—white fired clay—
cups, vases, water jars,
stacked high in dark chambers.
There was hardly discernment
between earth and horizon,
only the imagining
of a little green
to share with the goats stumbling around
for some pasture to lie down to.
What I wanted was to belong
to a space for us all,
something red and sweet to eat,
evidence of something
that could hold us all together here,
crushed grapes turned into wine
to drink with some beloved companion
I still wait for
but can't understand.

I Wander

down museum wings
click clock by sentinels
hallways passageways
to the gallery
of women dazing
through a hundred years
Portraits of ladies
staring from tufted couches
straight-backed chairs
at a fan at a distance
from a dish of plums
One's wrist hangs listlessly
her white dress cinched at the waist
with a black velvet line
She has forgotten the name of her
last admirer
One's chin rests on a cupped hand
her dress ruffled at the neck
She holds the table and a cigarette
imagining the dresses
in the shop across the street
Still life madams
stare through corridors
through artists going on
along horizontal lines
of bored perspective
until I stop at Joan

    whose eyes have found some parallel in space
    one hand stretched to grasp a branch
    to hold it taut between strong fingers the
    other clenched for something rough like
    the texture of her skirt
    The weedy forest calls her name her eyes
    shocked search some distance
    for the place to light her soul

Sanctum

I
*Mary Magdalen bused a pushcart of sins
to the front of my house.
I wiped my palms on my skirt
and signed for them.
They came in truckloads after that,
backed in at the porch door,
by wet clothes lying in a laundry basket.
Put them over there, I said,
and they piled higher and higher,
brown packages in twine.
My kids made forts from the boxes,
igloos through the kitchen,
UPS cartons in a maze
all the way to the washing machine.*

II
Mary Magdalen's body lies in pieces
all over France.
An arm in Normandy is wrapped in silk,
the other lies at St. Maximin's.
Louis VIII had five hairs and a bone;
A sarcophagus, it is said,
holds her body at Vezelay,
complete, but for a leg.
Francois I carried off her head
as a gift for his Queen.
I wish I'd been at court in 1515
to see the king
lift it to the audience
a reliquary
holding her skull.

In Spain, a monastery claims her hair.
Someone gave a finger to a pope.

It's hard to think of my friend as a body part,
a charm for a celibate priest.
I have packages from her myself,
her lace stockings.
If they should find out, a mob,
the multitudes, would trample me.

I remember the day she met him: Christ!

She'd gotten into trouble
hanging around creeps,
the kind who drag you by the neck
into newspapers, glossy mags,
TV clips of motels and courtrooms.

But as long as He was there, no one touched her,

not a finger,
not a hair.

She followed him faithfully,
not aimlessly,
like the men burnt out
from flashbulbs and cigarettes,
sores all over their flesh.
In the end, He left her looking like a saint.
She came home
smelling of musk, of damp earth;
her bare feet left sweet oil
prints all over the floor.

Women Writers

> *We starve without poetry. It is the possibility of rejuvenation.*
>
> —Maya Angelou

We used to sit in circles to quilt,
take Tupperware orders.
We braided rugs, knit wool socks.
I had a Tupperware party once.
We ordered green plastic spoons
while my daughter
fell down a flight of stairs.
These days we heave deep nets,
 light torches to feverish brains,
our brains,
write in circles
pull paper over knees, and write
stories of our ancestors, family trees.
We write about the blood between us.
We stain the sofa, like old wine,
vinegar, and earth.
We write about sweating at night,
broken up between full moons,
and children gone off to college.
Our bodies we carry out in bulrush baskets.
After the flood, after we reach shore, we
get up out of them, finally,
and become queens.

Mountain Legend

In the distance lies a sleeping giant
frozen for his jealousy and greed.
I try to find his eyes, his mouth
his ears to whisper in:
Have some mercy for yourself and live.
He takes up the sky for miles,
makes it dark too soon,
casts long shadows for us
living near his side.
When I undress for bed,
I think of his chest, his legs,
imagine I am large enough
to lie in the crook of his neck,
warm him, prop up his head, sing to him,
and we could have some peace by spring.
I dream of his waking.
I fall from his face, fall
to a heap, my own arms and legs
sprawled out for wolves to tear,
gag down their hungry winter throats.
One by one they appear, the tricksters
wink to each other and move in.
But they only hiss, warn me.
If the giant moves
little houses fall over like game board pieces,
plastic red and green,
ringing from his ledges like goat bells.
A man at supper rumbles back his chair,
one arm high in the air, a spoon in his hand.
His wife looks up in horror.
All the hauling it took to build up there
along the curve of his shoulder
down the front of his stomach
furry with trees!

Lights

I wasn't invited by the Magis
in the first place. No one showed me
the star, least of all myself.
No wash of purple and midnight
called me out to desert vigil
where bright angels
might have startled me
singing their marvelous poetry.
No one called me to the window,
wove chocolate into my dreams,
flirted with my girlish feet in ballet slippers.
There never were carolers on the street
outside, snowy with white of dreams,
although I wanted them to come
so desperately.
I bought ceramic figures later,
I guess in my thirties. They stood mute
around bowls of ribbon candy while I wished
Jesus would change the whole world.
But the string of lights,
big bulbs of garish red and blue
brought down from my mother's attic,
lying in Stonehenge formation on the floor,
said in the truth of their plugging in and working
some twenty-five years later:
Behold the circle from the sleepy child you were,
Bright again, bright again!
Dance with us through green winking branches;
We are the reason for everything.

3.

Elegy for Laverne

From somewhere in the middle of the night,
the jewels came,
heaped over the quilt, the cats,
my sleeping husband.
I saw them by streetlight;
mounds of ruby blue lay on the pavement
between apartment buildings,
shattered diamonds banked up by the curbs.
There had been a funeral that day,
its slow caravan unraveled
like black ribbon through town.
Were these clues from the dead,
something from the place he had reached,
the many mansions?
Or things that from morning stoops,
early women scoop up like seashells,
know as trail marks through the city
to some refreshing end,
a waterfall?
I saw them only once,
a year ago July.
I remember their weight on my covers,
their sparkle on the lawn outside.
Towards morning a wind came up,
and they were gone. But last night,
just as air turned to late summer
in my sleep,
I heard a rush like glassy stones
sliding from a huge, magnificent sky.

In the Beginning

We thought all the houses would
nestle together brightly,
learn to sing together in the winter,
and let the wide cold outdoors surround us
with white, snowy fields.
In the beginning, I didn't mind being the one to go into town
only to get food.
In the beginning, spring was a sure thing,
not like now when it seems like we're stuck here,
in this outpost, no words from home,
not one crackle on the phone lines,
the radio dead.
Yes, a sure thing. You could joke about it,
spring being just around the corner and all that.
In the beginning, birth starts fast.
They scurry about you,
your breathing and heartbeats splash on hospital monitors.
Amniotic fluids swish loud, *it's happening*.
Then black birth canal narrows,
presses on deep bones.
You lose your nerve, slow down.
No exit. Stone cold.

For David and Megan

Yesterday, I followed home
a yellow school bus
threading its way through town.
Each stop
became a one-act play,
a pantomime in my windshield,
the windshield wipers back and forth,
a background music.
A mother waits beneath her umbrella.
The dog sitting at her feet stares at the school bus door.
The door opens. He yanks, a boy pops out,
the wild leash spins them all together, laughing.
A little girl, her full skirt
opened like a parasol,
hops to the ground,
runs down a long driveway,
jumps into happy arms at the end.

We remember our own gifted days
when you kept opening and slamming doors—
the refrigerator, the cupboards—hollering for food
and more attention,
while that background music,
the singing of our families,
twirled and twirled you
into today.

Take with you, when you leave
for your own front porch,
what we all did together raising you.
Some pictures of the prom,
the fireplace, white tablecloths at Christmas,
a flock of running terns at Nauset,
and that one of Nana holding you.
Whichever window keeps the light

to look back in,
see your families watching you
in the little rowing boat that holds you both
under a sunny canopy,
making your own way home.

Letting Go

> *Your children are not your children.*
> *They are the sons and daughters of Life's longing for itself.*
> *They come through you but not from you,*
> *And though they are with you, yet they belong not to you.*
>
> — *Kahlil Gibran*

Give them soft,
give them lovers in flowers
with big sighs, freckled eyes, and laughing lashes.
When the pyre of my motherhood
burns down the house behind me,
when I hang my children from the window
and it's time to jump or let them go,
when my fingers open and they drop,
curled, milk-bubbled, and falling down
in their buntings with birds and ducks and crescent moons,
as they slip from my arms, my dreams,
and I lean out screaming
Watch out! My children are falling!
when my hands are palm-open in fright,
my vision rent by a car speeding between us,
just when I was about to tell them something like
Don't ever leave me!
let there be grace:
wide, and fortunate blue.

For Nickels and Candy

I found coins littered all over the house—
one in the oven even,
and on a stair (had she sat down there?)
in her brother's crib;
by the cat's dish too, as if paying the tab
for his meal.
Not a concern, really;
better than pennies.
Nickels were rewards
but apparently worthless.
Candy works better, my mother said.
Candy kept my son's language clean
at school. Who could know a five-year-old
would convey such rattling images at daycare?
Who could know my little girl
would need rewards for using
indoor plumbing rather than the backyard?
In my old age, I smile to see
silver buffaloes and Snickers bars,

and remember tousled hair.

Advice For My Teenager

My son lit a firecracker
through his open window.
It rushed back in and around his room,
started a fire on his rug.
You fool! I said, you could've burned
like college boys in their beds!
Mattresses blaze up in twenty minutes
after sparks settle down and nest in cotton.
They gather momentum then agree,
every one of them in the dark behind your back,
to explode! When you're on the phone
with your girlfriend and her rock and roll,
BOOM! Like an empty cereal box
tossed in a fireplace smokes a little,
turns brown, waits till you put your hand in,
then fire makers inside it
leap to circle wagons, implode at once
like stage lights, opening curtain, lift off!
And there's your stupid hand
stuck in the blazing building
you thought was only smoldering!

Amherst in Perspective

On graduation Sunday,
away from the traffic-choked town,
I'm in a meadow looking through binoculars
at Indigo Buntings, blazing sapphire and black,
their songs elegant as the breeze feels,
as the ripples look on the pond.
It's a wide field.
Apple blossoms in the distant orchards
have just barely gone by, white confetti on green.
High over it, swallows dip, wings perpendicular to sky.
The bird I'm watching on a fencepost now
watches me poke my way towards her
through early grass and new shoots of swamp maples.
In the distance church bells ring, a congregation sings a hymn;
further away, I hear faint rolls of cheers,
wave after wave from the UMass stadium,
and I think of my daughter, still young,
playing in the commencement orchestra,
under a tent, watching mortarboards fly,
her flute clear and vivid as black confetti against blue.

Barn Cats at Big Meadow Creek

We don't know what happened to the mother cat;
she must have crawled beneath the house.
A hawk or coyotes carried off half her litter,
but the three left are playing on the porch this morning,
a calendar day: wide yellow hills,
Idaho in July.
The kittens hop from flower baskets,
toss themselves into windy bushes, and fall out again,
play on the belly of the papa cat.
He grins, his eyelids droop
warm light takes the chill off his coat
and the scary part of night.
He rubs his spine, a spindle like a spool bed post,
up against my legs, winds himself around my lap, yawns,
and falls asleep.
Every living thing should be held under the sky in a warm sweater.
Everyone should have a time to remember
stretching arms out to the sun dreaming,
or nursing on the stomach of a mother while she's living,
while she's a place to need,
before she's gone beneath a house to smell like damp, open woods,
her body vacant, wet ground forming closure
to her wide, empty eyes.

For Sylvia Plath

As if she'd found poems
smear like the stamens of lilies,
leave a stain on your blouse like blood,
the grief of summer ending,
she left them to be the wife,
to work the country house,
to name flowers.
She twisted dough to perfect loaves,
cut tulips for dinner ghosts and lovers.
A hundred thousand daffodils gossiped
while her children, curled darlings,
slept in tall grass,
and her husband disappeared.
In the crackle of a bonfire,
she heard them again, her poems.
They seared her skin, cut veins in black marble,
bled down the bark of hurting trees.
She wrote them down, the blazing ones,
then lay like bread set down on bricks,
to rise white hot with words,
to rise from the centers
of foxglove, morning glory, larkspur.

After Easter

> *Every blade of grass has its angel that bends over it and whispers, "Grow, grow."*
> —*The Talmud*

She packed the car in a cold spring rain,
her hair wet, coat soaked,
No umbrella?
A waste of time, she said,
as if the rush of leaving
could stave off missing so much,
then swooped back in,
my own young ladybird,
grabbing boats, superheroes, trucks,
sneakers, boots, hats,
sorting mine from theirs,
and buckled the boys in the car.

I close the door,
half my wooden heart gone again,
and set to cleaning:
fold up cot, tie back curtains,
pull sheets off beds,
find strands of her hair beneath a pillow
and two hairpins,
three little boy socks,
a red car on the fireplace mantel.

The cats come out from hiding,
up from the cellar like some happy spring bulbs.
We walk in the yard as the sun comes out,
daffodils shrill with yellow.
Later, upstairs, to check on the lonesomeness,
I think of their kisses through car windows,
find strands of Easter basket grass everywhere:
in hall, bathtub, dresser drawers, rumpled blankets.
Green, strewn across whole rooms,
like a wide, dreamy lawn.

Spring Drowning

Three men in wetsuits
were diving with ropes below the dam
of Puffer's Pond last spring:
someone's boy was missing.
The father, his hands clenched in pockets,
stared down into roiling foam,
imagining his son's body
turning over and over in the falls.
The mother, crouched in a wool blanket,
tilted her head as if straining to hear a shout
from behind the roaring curtain:
Here he is! And he's fine!
His friends stomped feet in the raw morning,
remembering how warm the day had been,
how his body had gleamed in an arc to the water
in his dive.

I walked along the lower banks
of streams that run from the pond,
imagining a swell of sunken mass
in the dark reflections of overhanging trees.
But he couldn't be the weight of heavy fabric,
like soaking towels or stones in a sack.
He was bare that day,
light as boiled meat slipped from a bone.
For two days, they searched.
How does a corpse
spin along like leaves in running water
and get lost?

They pulled him from a deep place
where the spillage hits the rocks.
We are not our bodies,
I whisper in my dreams to his parents,
who wring their hands and tumble after him,
dark after dark,
spring after lonesome spring.

Missing

You hear pre-dawn leave-taking
rustling,
quick folding of things,
back porch steps
in careful staccato
going down up down,

out
to a low rumble of motor
mumbling
to get moving
before having to say
anything.

Listen:
the quiet afterward,
the no-one-there of house.

You can hear the missing, too,
in reluctant music after dinner,
the familiarity
missing
from the full matter
of his laughter

when you embraced him,

being careful
not to stay about him long,
the smell of mourning
in the quiet panic
of your clothes.

Ode to Losartan

White life button, charm
of pressured heart strings,
diastolic acoustic bass,
harmony with systolic,
your gig of cook
to high, hot blood
stills my own
iambic irregular
from a gallop
to a trot
to ordinary,
regular,
everyday life.

You Know

the hollow of a black moon
that has no face. You must be sweating
when you grope for a switch in the kitchen
at two a.m. Your feet scorch the freezing floor.
The room looks rotten-orange, dripping walls.
The cats cry, the dog pants by the back door.
Nothing is right.
A night train shudders somewhere. You wonder,
what freight goes out of here, what cargo?
Old tires? Clattering steel to some dirty shipyard?
All this because you are not sleeping.
You follow the animals to the yard.
Winter yanks at your bedclothes,
while you fight everything,
the coming day, its hostile work.
Outside are dead streets,
dark houses without eyes,
stiff garden skeletons.
You inhale wide, cold air.
You are breathing.
And look up:
Oh! The stars!

Trespasser

Trees were turning
into golds, fiery reds,
when out of the majesty of twilight,
before cold blue became an echo
of everything unfinished,
a gunshot blast.

The policeman's car radio sputtered.
I was just singing in the field like this,
I told him, and opened my arms like a blackbird,
flapping into silhouettes of branches in purple dusk.
I was singing for a congregation of pumpkins,
lines of them in pew-like furrows
when someone fired a shot.

I didn't shoot at her, the man said.
His wife was cooking supper;
his kids whirled around the cruiser like gnats.
*Nobody tells me I can't shoot
on my own land.*

I went back to the field today,
imagined a man sliding a red cartridge
into a steel barrel,
thought of buzzards circling above me.
My shoes loose from the wet marsh,
I dropped to take them off,
and lay back, singing again,
face-up to the ownerless sky.

Sacrificial Rites

We gave away our names sheepishly,
stupid as a frog
whose eyes are glazed over,
while its leg, caught in the beak of a hawk,
starts to vanish.
Who gives this woman to this man?
I do, said our fathers who took us down.
We left our names at an altar.
Do you see what I'm getting at?
Our identity, veiled in white,
dropped down like a ballgown,
unzipped,
to the floor.
Wine spilled on white,
stained permanently.
Insipid cherry metaphors
ground down our pride
in bad toasts at rehearsal dinners.
I like you but your damned names buried ours,
until some of us wandered,
took years "off" to find ourselves.
But we can't find each other.
We searched for decades, but
identities, spent in strange ceremony,
vanished.
The tongues of sisters, classmates,
sometimes soulmates,
were silenced, grafted onto a stranger's tree,
grew new names; limbs
were bound with wedding ribbons,
and the two were made one,
but I don't think so.
In old age I keep practicing my rite of absurdity,
searching them by the only names I had known:
the maiden names of Anne Katz from Chicago,

Margaret Schilling on Long Island,
Kathy Russell in Syracuse....
If reading this, you knew of them
and who they are today,
please tell them to find Susan Riley
under Kortright, Murphy, or Clarke.

Leaving P'town Before the Parade

*We are stardust, we are golden
and we've got to get ourselves
back to the garden.*

—Joni Mitchell

I followed a float up Route 6A,
a decorated hayride: bare boys
riding on top in raz-a-ma-taz bikinis,
grinning in flashy shades.
Lawn chairs staked out by roadsides,
crowds of ladies in rainbow everything
marched in from the outskirts.
But I was done, for the most part, driving home
before it all came down.
Leaving this curl of land in shining
end-of-summer seas, I'm nostalgic.
But I'm not one for crowds.
Up on Route 6, I passed car after car
two solid lanes backed up for miles:
stuffed station wagons, Ford pick-ups,
flashy convertibles, money like confetti
flying out of them.
By the time they'd get to Ptown,
they'd be half a million strong,
like Joni's Woodstock song.
You'd have to want to be there bad
to wait in a nine-mile backup, I thought,
but then it dawned on me:
O'er the ramparts, the flag still there.
They were coming to witness immense longing,
to celebrate new freedom,
everyone rising up, clamoring as it grew.
I flashed back to a photograph of New York State Thruway,
jammed for miles, August 15, 1969.
I wasn't there, neither was Joni,
but this became a universal chant:
Yes you were! It's a state of mind!

A Change in Luck

Any minute now something will happen
the windshield wiper said on her way
driving in the rain. She turned the radio down
to channel the thought, the idea,
the bright light in her hoping.
She turned it off so she could hear the voice
when it came to her. She will hear it any minute
it will come like the hill in the distance,
watershed washing down the pavement,
closer into viewpoint, then it will happen,
there will be strong direction in the voice
as if you could locate a distant friend in the rush
of a Trailways station after twenty years
without a letter or a Christmas card beforehand.
It will come like a piece of white lined paper
twisted around the branch of a pine tree
on the side of the dirt road in back of your house.
It says Judith Cranston, 1835 North Elm Street,
with a phone number. You call and she says yes
I've been waiting for you; I have a message to give you.
Any minute it will come upon you as the blue Comet
in the bathtub turns dark, and greasy rivulets melt away.
Any time now the patches in the highway form rubrics
and a phone ringing the right amount of rings gets answered
by the one who was expecting the very same call.
If you know anyone who passed through that time
I will offer them my life's savings.
For such a one I have waited all my life.
I read stories about them
I am faithful by the pool of Bethsaida,
but even though I watch figures and ripples in the rainwater
I see in my rear mirror, going sixty,
a driver roll down her window and reach around,
sun blinding her vision, to pull a leaf
from the wiper blade of her windshield.
Her car careens back and forth across the yellow line,
in her other hand that steers the wheel, a cigarette.
Do we crash or drown?

Off Across the Bay

on a spring night
lights spin in and out
like fish eyes
staring—dart off
focus—blur
surface—flutter
reflections of the mooring lantern ripple down about the rocks
bells somewhere in the harbor
back and forth ring darkly
a hollow foghorn sighs
it's been one whole year since you left

And the shells
bridge on chambers
paint out pink ceilings
archways rings of catacombs
the ones who wait at seaside
step in spirals
fumble prayer beads
darn fingernails
there are litanies in your name

I watch the bay from here
for one last wave to start my row

You Linger

twisted
speechless
suffocating
beg delivery into white
beg
how could this be
all of
you
disappear
before Nauset
for one more day
sand shovels, Cheez-its
Eli's sneaker in the parking lot

one can't hold back
wild grief rampant
open the freezer
blueberries
we picked last summer
everywhere shared
books music
floods space
a wild savage this grief
devours
a whole life
we
showed up in together
again
and again
the same beautiful story

Time of Death

All of us will lose our lives,
but bring us something from before
to light us home.
A deer, a sparrow
by the edge of the window,
a phone call in the dark
to tell us *This war is over!*
We are liberated!
Could we have a little year
to finish up,
open a musky cottage in the summer,
put flowers by the door,
spread out strawberries with white napkins,
drink champagne with dear friends?
Might we wrap ourselves once more
in soft towels at the beach,
after sailing on cold blue Cape Cod water,
flying in the wind ahead of time,
before it comes to us
that this has been our life?
This is it.
This is heaven.
It comes to us
like the memory
of a matterless sigh.

ACKNOWLEDGMENTS

Gratefully acknowledged are the following publications, where certain poems first appeared in earlier versions:

"Holding the Moon", *River Oak Review*

"The Interview", "Women Writers", *Willa: A Journal of the Women's Issues in Literacy*

"At Kenyon July 24", *The Midwest Quarterly*

"Georgia O'Keefe", *English Journal*

"For John Lennon", *Peregrine*

"Train Platform", *River Oak Review*

"Sweet Corn", *Women's Sojourner*

"First Marriage", *Slant*

"Elegy for Laverne", *Primavera*

"Amherst in Perspective", "Leaving P'town Before the Parade", *Cape Cod Times*

"Barn Cats at Big Meadow Creek", *Lullwater Review*

"You Know" (as "For Christine"), *Schuylkill Valley Journal*

"A Change in Luck", *Denver Quarterly*

* * *

With my deepest gratitude I'd like to thank Rebecca Kinzie Bastian, Susan's and my editor. Through sheer love and kindness she worked endlessly to edit and organize my mother's work. She also taught me so much about the beautiful world of writing and publishing. Her impressions and teachings have truly changed me and will last more than a lifetime. Also, from the bottom of my heart, I'd like to thank Cornerstone Press, most specifically Dr. Ross Tangedal (director and publisher), Karlie Harpold (editor), and Allison Lange (cover designer). They truly make the world more beautiful. Thank you for appreciating the value and beauty of my mother's writing. Because of you, I can share Susan's story, craft, and messages with the rest of the world. And lastly, thank you to all of Susan's friends, colleagues and former students for supporting Susan and me in this process. We are forever grateful!

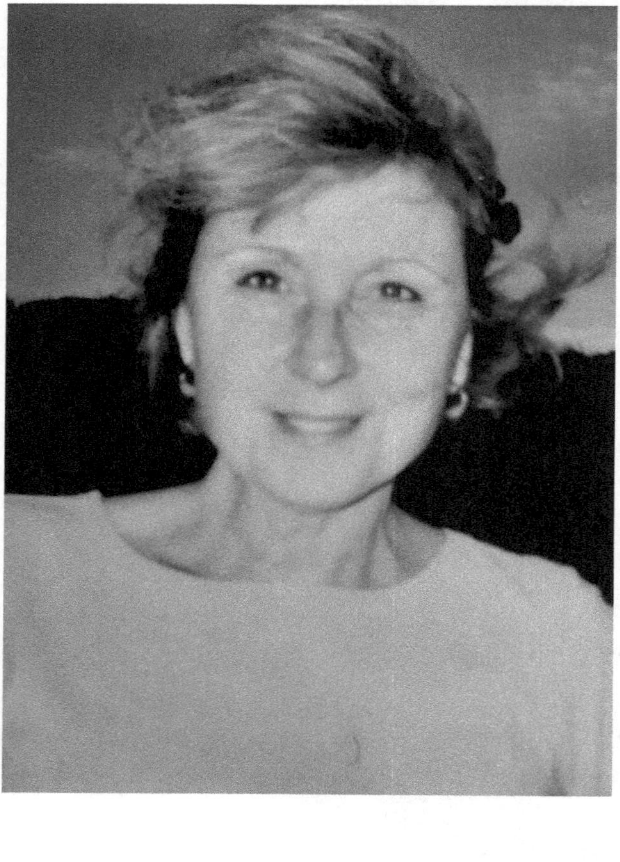

Susan Riley Clarke was an educator and freelance writer from Massachusetts, where she lived for most of her life. Born in Westford, she raised her children in Amherst and enjoyed her retirement in South Yarmouth. Susan spent a number of years in Connecticut, where she was an associate professor in the School of Education at Quinnipiac University. She was known to her friends, family, and colleagues for her sense of flair, her purposeful and artful use of words, her advocacy for equity and justice, her warmth for children, nature, and animals, and her love of the communities and beaches of Cape Cod. *Another Native Tongue* is a posthumous collection, as Susan died unexpectedly in her sleep in 2022.